A Guide for Using

Little House on the Prairie

in the Classroom

Based on the novel written by
Laura Ingalls Wilder

This guide written by **Linda Lee Maifair**

Teacher Created Materials, Inc.
6421 Industry Way
Westminster, CA 92683
www.teachercreated.com
©1995 Teacher Created Materials, Inc.
Reprinted, 2003
Made in U.S.A.
ISBN-1-55734-539-2

Illustrated by
Kathy Bruce

Cover Art by
Agi Palinay

Table of Contents

- ❖ Quiz Time!
- ❖ Hands-On Project — *Moving: Then and Now*
- ❖ Cooperative Learning Activity — *Little Houses on the Table*
- ❖ Curriculum Connection — Writing: *Whew!*
- ❖ Into Your Life — *Reading Response Journals*

- ❖ Quiz Time!
- ❖ Hands-On Project — *Block Party*
- ❖ Cooperative Learning Activity — *Wolf Watch*
- ❖ Curriculum Connection — Geography: *Little Houses Where?*
- ❖ Into Your Life — *Family Traits*

- ❖ Quiz Time!
- ❖ Hands-On Project — *Who Put Out the Candle?*
- ❖ Cooperative Learning Activity — *Yippi Ti Yi Yea!*
- ❖ Curriculum Connection — Social Studies: *Indian Camp*
- ❖ Into Your Life — *Dear...*

- ❖ Quiz Time!
- ❖ Hands-On Project — *Paper Prairie People*
- ❖ Cooperative Learning Activity — *Game Plan*
- ❖ Curriculum Connection — Health: *Emergency!*
- ❖ Into Your Life — *Chapter X*

- ❖ Quiz Time!
- ❖ Hands-On Project (Science) — *Little Garden on the Window Ledge*
- ❖ Cooperative Learning Activity — *Fire!*
- ❖ Curriculum Connection — Social Studies: *Geronimo!*
- ❖ Curriculum Connection — Writing: *Details, Details!*
- ❖ Into Your Life — *"The Only Good Indian"*

Introduction

A good book can touch our lives like a good friend. Within its pages are words and characters that can inspire us to achieve our highest ideals. We can turn to it for companionship, recreation, comfort, and guidance. It also gives us a cherished story to hold in our hearts forever.

In Literature Units, great care has been taken to select books that are sure to become good friends!

Teachers who use this literature unit will find the following features to supplement their own valuable ideas.

- A Sample Lesson Plan

- Pre-reading Activities

- A Biographical Sketch and Picture of the Author

- A Book Summary

- Vocabulary Lists and Vocabulary Activity Ideas

- Chapters grouped for study, with each section including:
  —*quizzes*
  —*hands-on projects*
  —*cooperative learning activities*
  —*cross-curriculum connections*
  —*extensions into the reader's own life*

- Post-reading Activities

- Book Report Ideas

- Research Ideas

- Culminating Activities

- Three Different Options for Unit Tests

- A Bibliography of Related Reading

- An Answer Key

We are confident that this unit will be a valuable addition to your planning and hope that as you use our ideas, your students will increase the circle of "friends" that they can have in books!

Sample Lesson Plan

Each of the lessons suggested below can take from one to several days to complete.

LESSON 1

- Introduce and complete some or all of the pre-reading activities found on page 5.
- Read "About the Author" with your students. (page 6)
- Read the book summary with your students. (page 7)
- Introduce SECTION 1 vocabulary list and ask students to find definitions. (page 8)

LESSON 2

- Read Chapters 1 through 5. As you read, place the vocabulary words in context and discuss their meanings.
- Choose a vocabulary activity. (page 9)
- Compare moving, then and now. (page 11)
- Begin house building project. (page 12)
- Explore point of view. (page 13)
- Begin "Reading Response Journals." (page 14)
- Administer SECTION 1 quiz. (page 10)
- Introduce SECTION 2 vocabulary list and ask students to find definitions. (page 8)

LESSON 3

- Read Chapters 6 through 10. Place vocabulary words in context and discuss their meanings.
- Choose a vocabulary activity. (page 9)
- Design quilt patch. (page 16)
- Research wolves. (page 17)
- Explore geography/map connections. (page 18)
- Identify character and family traits. (page 19)
- Administer SECTION 2 quiz. (page 15)
- Introduce SECTION 3 vocabulary list and ask students to find definitions. (page 8)

LESSON 4

- Read Chapters 11 through 15. Place vocabulary words in context and discuss their meanings.
- Choose a vocabulary activity. (page 9)
- Do candle experiment. (page 21)
- Learn a prairie song. (page 22)
- Explore social studies connections. (page 23)
- Write a letter for Ma and yourself. (page 24)
- Administer SECTION 3 quiz. (page 20)
- Introduce SECTION 4 vocabulary and ask students to find defintions. (page 8)

LESSON 5

- Read Chapters 16 through 20. Place vocabulary words in context and discuss their meanings.
- Choose a vocabulary activity. (page 9)
- Make paper prairie people. (page 26)
- Make up a game for Laura and Mary. (page 27)
- Explore health connections. (page 28)
- Write an autobiographical chapter. (page 29)
- Administer SECTION 4 quiz. (page 25)
- Introduce SECTION 5 vocabulary list and ask students to find definitions. (page 8)

LESSON 6

- Read Chapters 21 through 26. Place vocabulary words in context and discuss their meanings.
- Choose a vocabulary activity. (page 9)
- Grow a little garden. (page 31)
- Compare fire prevention, then and now. (page 32)
- Research and write a speech. (page 33)
- Explore the writing connection. (page 34)
- Explore prejudice. (page 35)
- Administer SECTION 5 quiz. (page 30)

LESSON 7

- Discuss any questions your students may have about the story. (page 36)
- Assign book reports and research projects. (pages 37 and 38)
- Display little house models begun in lesson 2.
- Choose culminating activity/activities. (pages 39 to 42)

LESSON 8

- Administer Unit test(s) of choice. (pages 43, 44, and 45)
- Discuss test answers and possibilities.
- Discuss student enjoyment of the book.
- Provide a list of related reading for your students. (page 46)

Before the Book

Before you begin reading *Little House on the Prairie* with your students, do some pre-reading activities to stimulate interest and enhance comprehension. Here are some activities that might work well in your class:

1. Predict what the story might be about just from hearing the title.

2. Predict what the story might be about just from looking at the cover illustration.

3. Discuss other books by Laura Ingalls Wilder that students may have heard about or read. (Examples: *Little House in the Big Woods, Farmer Boy, On the Banks of Plum Creek, By the Shores of Silver Lake, The Long Winter,* and *Little Town on the Prairie.*)

4. Answer these questions:
    - Are you interested in . . .
        . . . a story about a real family?
        . . . a story about pioneer times?
        . . . a story about life in America more than a hundred years ago?
    - Have you ever . . .
        . . . wondered what it was like to travel in a covered wagon?
        . . . gone on a special outing with a parent?
        . . . had to move away from a place you liked?

5. Predict the hardships that a family might encounter . . .
    . . . making a journey by covered wagon.
    . . . building a house and starting a farm on the prairie.
    . . . living by themselves miles from the nearest neighbor or town.
    . . . living in Indian Territory in the late 1800's.

6. Make a list of the skills and traits it would take to be a good pioneer. Add to this list as you read the book.

7. Work in groups or as a class to write your own story about life in pioneer days.

8. Write or read a story about a Native American child living on the prairie at the same time Laura Ingalls Wilder writes about in *Little House on the Prairie.*

9. Working in small groups, make a list of things you would take with you if you were a pioneer packing your wagon to travel to the prairie. Then, as a class, discuss the items on the lists. As you read, compare the class lists to what the Ingalls family actually had with them.

10. Ask what students would do today in one of these situations. Then, read the book to see what the Ingalls family did.
    - Your vehicle is caught in a flash flood.
    - Your dog is missing.
    - Your whole family is sick.
    - Your chimney catches on fire.
    - A wildfire threatens your home.
    - The government threatens to take your home and land.
    - You find yourself surrounded by a pack of wild animals.

About the Author

Laura Ingalls Wilder's books are based on the real experiences of her life. She once said, "I lived everything that happened in my books. It is a long story, filled with sunshine and shadow..."

She was born in the "little house in the big woods" in Pepin, Wisconsin, on February 7, 1867. In the 1870's the family moved several times, traveling by covered wagon from Wisconsin to Kansas to Minnesota and finally to the Dakota Territory. At the age of 15, she started teaching in a country school in DeSmet, South Dakota. She married Almanzo Wilder in 1885, and her daughter Rose, also an author, was born in 1886.

Her first "little house" book, *Little House in the Big Woods*, was published in 1932, when Laura Ingalls Wilder was 65 years old. She was surprised at the interest in what she thought were merely "family stories."

> "When to my surprise the book made such a success and children all over the United States wrote to me begging me for more stories, I began to think what a wonderful childhood I had had. How I had seen the whole frontier, the woods, the Indian country of the great plains, the frontier towns, the building of railroads in wild, unsettled country, homesteading and farmers coming in to take possession. I realized that I had seen and lived it all."

From 1932 to 1943, Laura Ingalls Wilder wrote eight "Little House" books in order to share those experiences with modern children.

> "I wanted children now to understand more about the beginning of things, to know what is behind the things they see — what it is that made America as they know it."

In 1953, new editions of the books were published with illustrations by Garth Williams, who did extensive research and retraced the paths the Ingalls family took in their journeys through the frontier in order to make his illustrations as authentic as possible.

Laura Ingalls Wilder lived to be 90 years old. She died at Rocky Ridge Farm in Mansfield, Missouri, on February 10, 1957. She had lived through vast changes in America.

> "Today our way of living and our schools are much different; so many things have made living and learning easier. But the real things haven't changed. It is still best to be honest and truthful; to make the most of what we have; to be happy with simple pleasures and have courage when things go wrong."

(Quotations from *Something About the Author,* Gale Research Company.)

Little House on the Prairie
by Laura Ingalls Wilder

(Harper & Row, 1935, 1953)

(Available in Canada and Australia from HarperCollins; in UK from HarperCollins Publishers, Ltd.)

Have you ever had to move away from a place you liked and people you loved? When Laura Ingalls, her parents, and her sisters moved from Wisconsin to Kansas more than a hundred years ago, they had no automobiles or airplanes to travel in, no moving vans to haul their belongings, no fast food restaurants to eat in or motels to sleep in along the way, and no house waiting for them when they got there. There was no school, no other children to play with. The nearest town, store, and post office were forty miles away!

When Laura's father decided that Wisconsin was getting too crowded, he and his wife packed their children and their belongings into a covered wagon, leaving behind the furniture which was too big and heavy to take along. They traveled for weeks, riding all day. They washed their dishes and clothes in a bucket of water hauled from a nearby stream. Pa hunted for the food they ate on the way, and Ma cooked it over a campfire. They slept in the wagon, out on the open prairie, listening to the howl of wolves and with nothing but Pa's gun and their dog, Jack, to protect them. And the whole family nearly drowned trying to cross a flooded creek.

Finally, Pa found the place he wanted to build their new house and start their new farm. The girls did what they could to help as Ma and Pa built a log house and made it snug and comfortable by adding a door, a real roof, a fireplace, a chimney, and a wooden floor. They dug a well. They plowed the land and put in a garden. They made friends with their new "neighbors," other settlers like themselves who lived a few miles away. They survived a deadly fever and faced the threat of an Indian attack. And, through quick thinking and hard work, they saved their new home from a raging prairie fire.

But, after all they had been through — just when it looked like they would begin to live off the land they had worked so hard to settle — the government told them they would have to leave. By mistake, they had settled three miles over the line, in Indian Territory. Leaving behind their house and barn, their garden, and the plow in the field, the Ingalls family packed up their wagon again and moved on.

Little House on the Prairie is based on the real-life experiences of author Laura Ingalls Wilder. In reading the book, you will meet a girl who is much like you in many ways. You will also have a very good idea of what it might have been like to have been a pioneer child, traveling by covered wagon and trying to make a home on the prairie.

Vocabulary Lists

On this page are vocabulary lists which correspond to each sectional grouping of chapters. Vocabulary activity ideas can be found on page 9 of this book.

SECTION 1
(Chapters 1–5)

wandered	hunched	nickered
comfortable	briskly	tidy
jolting	muttered	vanished
hitch	ford	admired
brindle	hewed	savory
enormous	lurched	contentment
wonder	pulsing	foundation
flared	stealthily	huddled
bounded	crinkled	hobbled

SECTION 2
(Chapters 6–10)

scalawag	auger	rage
stout	scrambled	dashed
shuddered	saplings	sizzled
quavered	delicate	padded
vast	reprovingly	shied
pacing	splendid	notched
deserted	glittered	stout
beholden	radiance	murmured
hearth	amazed	anxiously

SECTION 3
(Chapters 11–15)

bedstead	trotted
disgrace	exclaimed
fierce	spattered
windlass	wavering
ravines	dwindling
objected	jabbered
parching	drawled
swiftly	luscious

SECTION 4
(Chapters 16–20)

sparing	limply
massacre	yonder
contradict	acquainted
rummaged	uncinched
sober	delicate
quivering	mournfully
squatted	bristled
interrupt	

SECTION 5
(Chapters 21–26)

coaxed	cautiously	ornery
patient	devilment	sensible
jubilation	muffled	snugly
surly	stockade	brood
sod	terror	meekly
billowing	placid	scorched
staggering	gazed	furious

Vocabulary Activity Ideas

You can help your students learn and retain the vocabulary in *Little House on the Prairie* by providing them with interesting vocabulary activities. Here are a few ideas to try.

- Have students make their own **Crossword Puzzles** or **Wordsearch Puzzles.** Make copies of the completed puzzles so students can exchange them.

- Make an illustrated **Pioneer Life Dictionary** in which students illustrate, define, and provide a simple context sentence for vocabulary words related to pioneer life and for other pioneer terms and devices in the book.

- Challenge your students to a **Vocabulary Bee.** This is similar to a spelling bee, but students must both spell and define each word correctly.

- Put all the vocabulary words in a box. Have each student or pair of students draw six words from the box. Give the students or student pairs a time limit of 15 minutes (or whatever time appropriate for your group) to write a **Short Vocabulary Story,** incorporating all six words drawn and using them correctly.

- Play **Vocabulary Charades.** In this game, vocabulary words are acted out.

- Play **Vocabulary Football.** Draw a football field, with yard lines, on the blackboard. Divide the class into two teams. Play starts at the 50-yard line. A toss of the coin decides which team "receives" first. The teacher gives a vocabulary word to a member of the receiving team. If he/she defines it correctly, the ball (a chalk "X", an oaktag football with sticky tape on the back, etc.) is moved 10 yards toward that team's goal. A missed word is a fumble, and the other team receives. Each "touchdown" is 6 points.

- Play **Synonym Relay.** Each row (equal number of students) is a team. The teacher calls out a word. The first person in the row writes one synonym for the word and then passes the paper back to the next person. He/she adds a second synonym and passes the paper back to the third person, and so on. The winning team is the first to finish the list with correct (no repetition) synonyms for the vocabulary word.

- Have students make **Flash Cards** for each vocabulary word, writing the word on the front and the definition on the back. They can then practice in pairs or small groups, showing the word and asking for the definition or showing the definition and asking for the word. Flash cards can also be taken home for additional practice and review.

- Make one vocabulary word each day the **Word of the Day.** Write the word on the chalkboard. Students, collectively, earn a point each time someone in the class uses the word correctly in a writing assignment, conversation, etc. You can establish a reward—like a free reading—period when the class accumulates a certain number of points.

You probably have many more ideas to add to this list. Try them! See if experiencing vocabulary on a personal level increases your students' vocabulary interest and retention.

Quiz Time!

1. On the back of this paper, write a one-paragraph summary of the major events in each chapter of this section. Then complete the rest of the questions on this page.

2. Why did Pa decide to leave the Big Woods? _____

    _____

3. Why did the Ingalls family not take their beds and tables with them when they moved?

    _____

4. Why were they in a hurry to get across the lake?

    _____

    _____

5. List four chores that Ma and Pa had to do when they made camp each night.

    A. _____

    B. _____

    C. _____

    D. _____

6. How did Pa solve the problem of getting the heavy logs to the top of the walls of the house?

    _____

7. What did Laura find when she went exploring?

    _____

8. Identify (explain who they are) each of these characters:

    A. Pet and Patty: _____

    B. Mr. Edwards: _____

    C. Jack: _____

9. What special talent did Mr. Edwards have that Laura admired?

    _____

    _____

10. The Ingalls family still have a lot of hard work ahead of them. On the back of this paper, make a list of the things they will still have to do to get their new farm settled and started.

Moving: Then and Now

Just like the Ingalls, families today often have to move. But moving today is a lot different from the days when Laura and her family moved. The sentences on the left describe moving in Laura's day. On the right, write statements that describe moving today.

Moving in Laura's Time	Moving Today
1. The family didn't know exactly where they were headed and had to build their own house when they got there.	
2. The family traveled by covered wagon.	
3. The family had to leave furniture and many of their belongings behind.	
4. The trip took many weeks or months.	
5. The family camped at night sleeping in or near the wagon.	
6. The family carried or hunted its food and cooked it over a campfire.	
7. The family did the laundry in water hauled from a creek and dried the clothes by laying them out on the grass.	
8. Some of the dangers the family faced were wild animals, flooded creeks, Indian attacks, and horse thieves.	
9. The trails were rough, and creeks and rivers had to be crossed by fording or floating the wagons.	
10. The family saw few if any other travelers on their journey.	

Little Houses on the Table

Pa and Ma and their neighbor Mr. Edwards worked together to build the little house on the prairie. Work together with some of your classroom "neighbors" to build a model of the little house in the book.

Step One: Decide what materials you will use and list them below. (For example, you can build your cabin from twigs, Styrofoam "logs" an empty cardboard box, etc. And you will need something to build it on, hold it together, and decorate or color it when you are through.

Step Two: Laura Ingalls Wilder listed all the steps Pa went through in building their house. List the steps you will have to go through to build your model. Check each item off when it is done.

Step Three: On a windowsill or table, display your model with those made by your classmates. Compare the ways the houses were built. Decide which model looks most like the house in the book.

Materials

_____

_____

_____

_____

_____

_____

_____

_____

Whew!

Little House on the Prairie is told from Laura's *point of view.* That means we are told Laura's side of things — the way she thinks and feels about what is happening. Suppose the book had been written from *Jack's* point of view? Put yourself in Jack's place and answer the following questions as *he* would answer them:

1. How did you feel about leaving your home in the Big Woods, Jack?

    _____

    _____

2. What was it like, making that long trip under the Ingalls' wagon?

    _____

    _____

3. You are very important to the Ingalls family, Jack. What do you think are your most important jobs or responsibilities?

    _____

    _____

4. How did you feel when you were trying to follow the Ingalls' wagon across the creek?

    _____

    _____

5. How did you feel when you found the family again?

    _____

    _____

6. Which member of the Ingalls family do you like best? Why?

    _____

    _____

Let Jack Tell It: The book does not tell us what happened to Jack between the time he swam into the creek and the time he showed up in camp. On a separate paper, tell what might have happened *from Jack's point of view.*

Reading Response Journals

One great way to insure that the reading of *Little House on the Prairie* touches every student in a personal way is to include the use of Reading Response Journals in your plans. In these journals, students can be encouraged to respond to the story in a number of ways. Here are a few ideas.

• Ask students to create journals for *Little House on the Prairie*. Initially, have them only assemble lined and unlined three-holed paper in a brad-fastened "book," with a blank page for the journal's cover. As they read the story, they may draw designs on the covers that help tell the story for them.

• Tell students the purpose of the journals is to record their thoughts, ideas, observations, and questions as they read *Little House on the Prairie.*

• Provide students with, or ask them to suggest, topics from the story that would stimulate writing. Here are a few examples from the chapters in SECTION 1.

— Compare Pa's idea of a place that's "too crowded" with the area where you live.

— How do you think Laura and Mary felt about having to move away from their grandparents, aunts and uncles, and cousins?

— How would you have felt? Have you ever had to make such a move? Write about it.

— Describe each member of the Ingalls family, the type of person you think each is. As you read the rest of the book add to or "correct" this first impression.

• After the reading of each chapter, students can write one or more new things they learned in the chapter.

• Ask students to draw their responses to certain events or characters in the story, using the blank pages in their journals.

• Tell students they may use their journals to record any "diary-type" responses they may want to enter.

• As they read, encourage students to jot down questions that come to mind about the story, the people, the events, or the time in which Laura lived. Discuss these questions in class, then allow students to record the answers in their journals.

• Encourage students to bring their journal ideas to life! Ideas generated from their journal writing can be used to create plays, debates, stories, songs, and art displays.

• Allow students time to write in their journals daily.

To evaluate the journals, you may wish to use the following guidelines:

— Personal reflections will be read by the teacher, but no letter grade will be given. Credit will be given for effort. All students who sincerely try will earn credit. If a grade is desired, grade according to the number of entries completed. For example, if five entries were required and a student conscientiously completed all five, he or she should receive an "A."

— Nonjudgmental, positive, and encouraging teacher responses should be made as you read the journals to let the students know that you are reading and enjoying them.

If you would like to grade student writing for form and content, ask the students to select one of their entries and "edit" it according to the writing process.

Quiz Time!

1. On the back of this paper, write a one-paragraph summary of the major events in each chapter of this section. Then complete the rest of the questions on this page.

2. In addition to Mr. Edwards, the Ingalls have two other sets of neighbors. Who are they and how far do they live from the Ingalls' house?

   (A) _____ miles away

   (B) _____ miles away

3. How did the bachelors solve the problem of deciding on whose land the house they were sharing should be built?

   _____

   _____

4. Describe the leader of the wolf pack that ran with Pa and surrounded their house.

   _____

   _____

5. What did Pa use to hold the chimney stones together? What was it made of?

   _____

   _____

6. What does stick-and-daub mean? Why did Pa have to build the top of the chimney that way?

   _____

   _____

7. What is it about Pa's looks that Ma often teases him about and that he even jokes about himself?

   _____

   _____

8. What prized possession did Ma put on the new mantle shelf?

   _____

   _____

9. How did Pa and Ma feel about getting the nails for their roof from Mr. Edwards?

   _____

   _____

10. On the back of this paper, write a paragraph that tells how the behavior expected of "good" children in Laura's time was different from the behavior allowed today.

Block Party

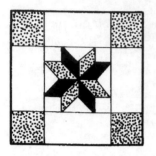

Quilts were very important to pioneer families. They not only kept them warm, they added a bit of color and decoration to their sparsely furnished homes. For recreation, Mary even prefers working on her quilt blocks to going outside with Laura. The illustrations on this page show two traditional quilt patterns that Mary, Laura, and Ma might have used.

Sometimes people embroidered their quilt blocks with flowers or other designs. Sometimes they embroidered them with pictures that represented someone or something special in their lives. In the space below, draw a design that you would put on a quilt block. The design should be something you like, something that represents you. (Examples: your pet, a slice of pizza or an ice cream cone, a basketball or a baseball bat, etc.)

Make a Real Quilt Block:

• Copy your design (above) on a 4" (10 cm) square of plain cloth.

• Use an embroidery needle and thread in your choice of colors to outline your design.

As an alternative, use scraps of colorful material to copy and sew together one of the traditional quilt designs at the top of the page.

Wolf Watch

In *Little House on the Prairie* Laura Ingalls Wilder tells about two frightening incidents with a pack of wolves. Write a one- or two-sentence summary of each incident below:

Pa's experience when he is out riding	
Laura's night time experience in the cabin	

From reading the story, you have learned several things about wolves and their habits. Working with a partner, fill in what you have learned on the chart below. Then look up wolves in an encyclopedia and add whatever new information you have found to your chart.

Wolves		
Appearance	**Habitat**	**Habits/Behavior**

Draw a picture of a wolf.

Little Houses Where?

Laura's family left Wisconsin and traveled to Kansas. They built their new house on the prairie in Indian Territory. Where, exactly, did they settle? What states did they cross? How big was Indian Territory? Use the novel, maps, history books, or encyclopedias to follow the instructions and finish the map below.

1. Draw a **red line** to show the route the Ingalls family traveled from Wisconsin to Kansas.

2. Fill in the names of all the present-day **states** they passed through on the way.

3. Draw a **star** to mark the location of the town of Independence, Kansas.

4. Draw **blue lines** to show the Mississippi, Missouri, and Verdigris Rivers.

5. Draw a miniature **house** to represent where the Ingalls family settled.

6. Shade the Indian Territory **green.**

7. Inside the shaded area, write the names of three Native American **tribes** who lived there.

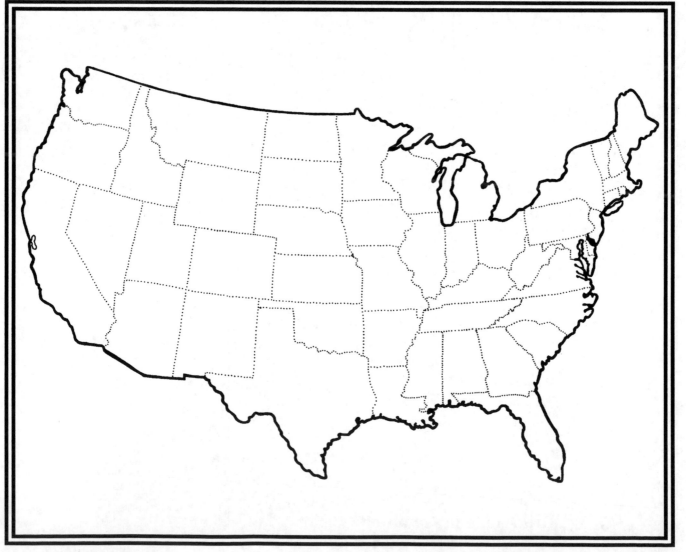

Family Traits

The diagram below is known as a Venn diagram. There are two circles. One circle is for Laura. The other circle is for her sister, Mary. The two circles overlap. In the part of Laura's circle on the left that does not overlap Mary's circle, make a list of words that describe Laura's behavior and personality but do not describe Mary. In the part of Mary's circle that does not overlap Laura's circle, list the traits that describe Mary but do not fit Laura. In the overlapping section in the middle of the diagram, list the traits that describe both Mary and Laura.

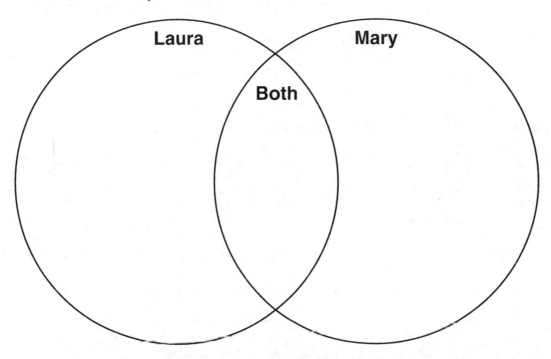

Do a similar Venn diagram for yourself and a member of your family — brother or sister, cousin, parent, grandparent, etc. Or do a diagram comparing you and one of your friends.

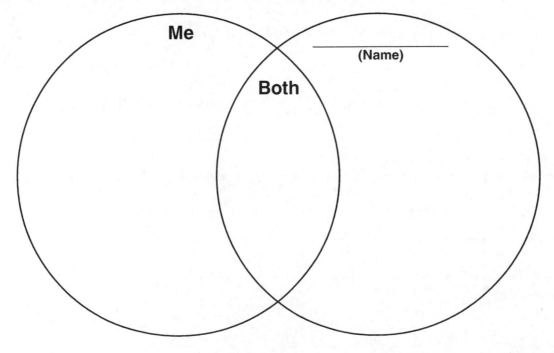

Quiz Time!

1. On the back of this paper, write a one-paragraph summary of the major events in each chapter of this section. Then complete the rest of the questions on this page.

2. Why did Ma give the Indians the cornbread and let them take Pa's tobacco?

   _____

3. What might have happened if the girls had disobeyed Pa and let Jack loose?

   _____

   _____

4. In what ways was the bed Pa and Ma made different from the beds we use today?

   _____

   _____

   _____

5. Why did Pa send a candle down the well each day before he went down to do more digging?

   _____

   _____

6. What happened when Mr. Scott did not listen to Pa's advice?

   _____

7. How did the cowboys pay Pa for the work he did for them?

   _____

8. Why was Laura upset about the beads she and Mary had found at the Indian camp?

   _____

9. What were the symptoms of the "fever 'n' ague" that nearly killed Laura and her family?

   _____

   _____

10. On the back of this paper, make a sketch of how you think the Indian camp looked when the Indians were there.

Who Put Out the Candle?

In Chapter 12 of *Little House on the Prairie*, Pa tells Mr. Scott, "Where a light can't live, I know I can't." Here is an experiment you can try to show you what he meant:

> **Materials Needed:**
> - small candle with candleholder
> - safety matches
> - glass jar taller than the combined height of the candle and candleholder
> - ashtray

Procedures:

1. Put the candle in the candleholder.

2. Use the match to light the candle.

3. Extinguish the match and put it in the ashtray.

4. Very carefully, set the glass jar, upside down, over the candle and candleholder. The opening of the jar should rest flat against the table.

Observations and Conclusions:

1. Describe what happens when the jar is put down over the lighted candle.

   _____

   _____

2. Remove the jar and repeat the experiment. What happens?

   _____

3. Draw a conclusion from your observations by completing the following statement.

   The candle cannot burn when _____

   _____

4. Why does the candle go out when it is covered by the jar?

   _____

   _____

5. Pa said, "Where a candle can't live, I know I can't." What do both Pa and the candle flame need to live? (Think about what the jar takes away from the flame.)

   _____

   _____

Yippi Ti Yi Yea!

Singing and music are mentioned throughout the book, *Little House on the Prairie*. Pa's fiddle playing is both a comfort and entertainment for Laura. It is a way for Pa and Mr. Edwards to relax after a hard day's labor. Even the cowboys and the Indians have their own songs. Here is your chance to learn one of those songs and teach it to your classmates! Then you can do what the Ingalls family and other people of their time did for fun long before TV, movies, and video games — get together and sing!

Work in groups of four or five for this project:

1. Find the lyrics and music for an old pioneer, cowboy, or translated Indian song that the group likes. This can be one of the songs mentioned in the novel or an old folk song like "Oh, Suzanna" or "My Darling Clementine" or "Bury Me Not On the Lone Prairie," etc. As soon as you have made your choice, let your teacher know what song you want to do. No two groups should do the same song.

2. Become familiar enough with the lyrics that you can teach them to your classmates. Find a place (hallway, cafeteria, etc.) where you can practice singing the song together.

3. Decide how you will accompany your song. Does one of your group play the piano, a guitar, or some other instrument? Can he/she play the melody? Can some (or all) of the members of your group tap or clap out the rhythm of the song while you sing? Can you locate a recording of the song that you could play for the class before you ask them to sing it? Practice again, using some kind of accompaniment.

4. Decide who will be your song leader. One person might lead the whole song while the others in the group sing behind him/her. Or, you might take turns, each member or a pair of members leading a different stanza of the song. Practice!

5. Have the teacher make enough copies of your song that you can give them to your classmates.

Sing Along Time! (Put the titles of all the songs in a box.)

6. If you have the space (outside in nice weather, in the gym, etc.) sit in a big circle, campfire style.

7. The teacher will draw one title at a time from the box. As your title is called, your group will pass out copies of your song, go to the "front" of the campfire, demonstrate your song, then lead the class in singing it once or twice. (If you know anything special about your song, share it with the group before you sing.)

Indian Camp

Pa takes Laura and Mary to explore the abandoned Indian camp. Laura Ingalls Wilder gives us a good description of what the camp was like after the Indians had gone. Look up one of the prairie Indian tribes in a book or encyclopedia. Then, in each box below, draw something Laura and Mary might have seen if they had gone to the Indian camp while the Indians were still living there.

Article of Clothing	Weapon or Tool
Home	**Animal**

Compare and Draw: Complete one or both of the following activities.

On a separate sheet of paper, make a similar chart, drawing something the Indian visitors would have seen when they went to the Ingalls' cabin.

On a separate sheet of paper, make a similar chart, drawing something Laura and Mary would see if they came to visit your town.

Dear...

The Ingalls' family has no idea where Laura and her family are or what has happened to them since they left the little house in the Big Woods. Now that Pa is making the long hard trip to Independence and the nearest post office, Ma can finally write her letter. On the lines below, write the letter you think Ma would write to her family in Wisconsin. Then, on a separate sheet of paper, write a letter to someone in your family. After your teacher has checked your assignment, put Ma's letter in your *Little House* folder or notebook and mail or deliver your other letter.

Dear Ma and Pa,

_____

_____

_____

_____

_____

_____

_____

_____

_____

_____

_____

_____

_____

Your loving daughter,

Caroline

Quiz Time!

1. On the back of this paper, write a one-paragraph summary of the major events in each chapter of this section. Then complete the rest of the questions on this page.

2. Sometimes, in an emergency, a person has the strength and courage to do things he/she would not be able to do ordinarily. Tell about a time Laura had such strength and courage.

   _____

   _____

3. How was sending and getting mail on the prairie different from sending and getting mail today?

   _____

4. Name three ways Mr. Edwards shows that he is a good neighbor.

   A. _____

   B. _____

   C. _____

5. What special gift did Pa bring Ma, Laura, and Mary from Independence?

   _____

6. What did the "old trail" Laura had found in the beginning of the book turn out to be?

   _____

7. What did Ma mean when she told Laura, "The plow and all our seeds for next year are in that bundle of furs?"

   _____

8. What Christmas traditions did the Ingalls family follow that many families still follow today?

   _____

   _____

9. What made the terrible scream that frightened the Ingalls family?

   _____

10. On the back of this paper, make a list for Pa to take to Independence. List all the errands he has to run and all the things he has to buy.

Paper Prairie People

Children who lived on the prairie, like Mary and Laura, had few toys. There were no fashion dolls and action figures or malls in which to buy them. The girls made their own dolls out of old paper, probably old newspaper or package wrapping paper. Make your own paper prairie person by following the directions below.

Directions:

1. Use the outline figure on the right as a pattern to cut your prairie person figure out of heavy paper.

2. Use separate construction paper, crayon-designed art paper, scraps of cloth, yarn (for hair and beards), etc., to make clothing and accessories for your choice of prairie person:

   A. Pioneer man or boy

   B. Pioneer woman or girl

   C. Indian woman or girl

   D. Indian man or boy

   E. Cowboy

3. Glue the clothing, hair, and other accessories to your figure. Draw in facial features.

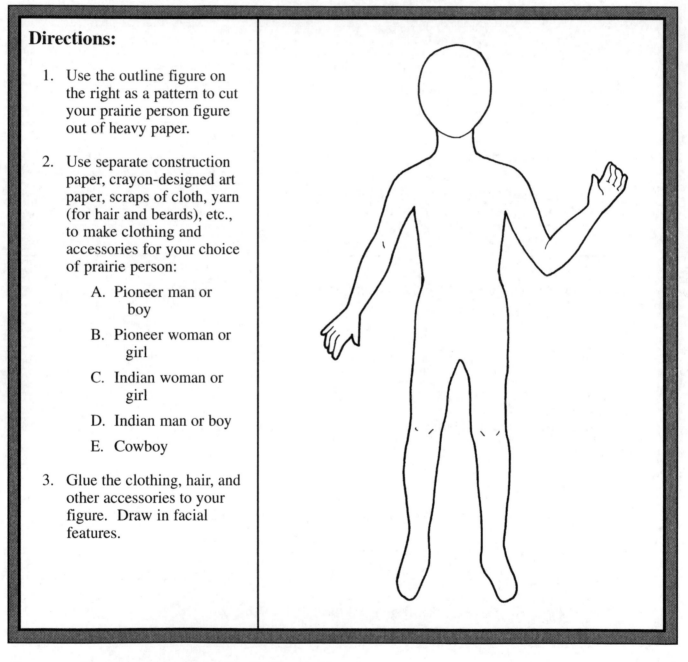

Here are a few ideas to try with your prairie people:

1. Display them along the border of a chalkboard or on a bulletin board.

2. Hang them in a row outside your classroom door so other classes can see them.

3. Get together in groups and write a short puppet skit to act out with your figures.

Game Plan

Mary and Laura play "Cat's Cradle" and "Hide the Thimble." What are your favorite games? Here are two games that have been favorites for many years. Play one or both with a classmate. Have fun!

"Cat's Cradle" Anyone?

Find someone — a classmate, a teacher, a friend or neighbor — who knows how to make a "cat's cradle" with string or yarn. Have that person demonstrate how it is done. (If necessary, use the illustration below as a guide.) Once you learn to do it, teach it to someone else — a classmate, brother or sister, or friend.

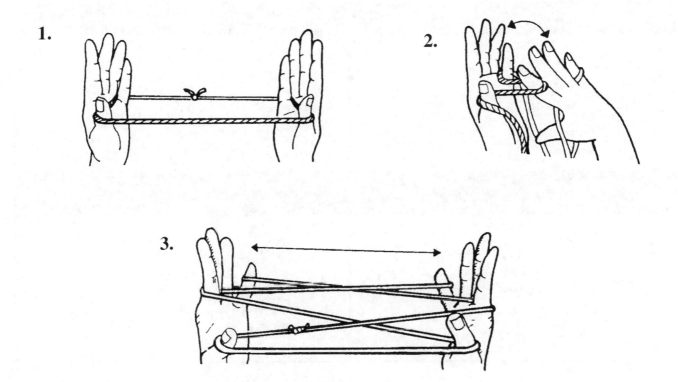

How About "Hide the Thimble"?

All Laura Ingalls Wilder tells us about this game is its name. Deduce (make logical assumptions about) how the game is played from the title. What do you think is the object of the game? What are the rules? What materials would you need to play?

You can play a version of "Hide the Thimble" with your classmates. Pairs of students take turns being "it." They leave the room long enough for their classmates to hide the thimble (or a chalk eraser, etc.) somewhere in the room. As a group, be sure to establish the rules and restrictions before you start. Must it be out in plain sight somewhere? Are any areas (like the teacher's desk) off limits? Then play a version of "20 Questions" when the pair who are "it" come back into the room. They ask up to 20 "yes" or "no" questions (such as "Is it on top of something?" or "Is it under anything?") before they have to make a guess where the thimble (or other object) is hidden. Then they rejoin the group and two new students are "it."

Emergency!

Pioneers had to be ready for any emergency. They could not run to the drug store. A doctor was not always available. They had to know what to do to help themselves, their families, and their neighbors.

In the left section of each block below, write in what the Ingalls family or their neighbors did about the emergencies they faced in the book. Then, invite your school nurse, a local doctor, an emergency medical technician, or someone trained in first aid to come to your class. Ask him/her what should be done in each case. Write his/her advice in the right section of each block below:

Someone has a badly sprained ankle.		Someone is overcome by toxic fumes.	
Someone has a very high fever.		**Someone is exposed to very cold temperatures and cold water.**	

Laura Ingalls Wilder does not tell us what they did after the prairie fire. How do you think they treated any burns Ma and Pa might have had on their hands? How do you think they soothed the girls' eyes and throats which had been bothered by the smoke? Ask your guest what you should do in these emergencies:

How to treat burns	How to treat eyes/throat irritated by smoke

Chapter X

Laura Ingalls Wilder's books are autobiographical. *Auto* is a prefix meaning self. A *biography* is a story written about a real person. An *autobiography* is a story about a person's life written by that person. In *Little House on the Prairie* and other books like *Little House in the Big Woods,* Laura Ingalls Wilder tells the story of her own life and family and the things they did as pioneers. For example, one of the chapters in *Little House on the Prairie* tells the story of a very special Christmas.

Suppose you were going to write an autobiography and one chapter of that book was going to be about a special holiday or celebration. Now, answer these questions:

1. What was the holiday or occasion of the celebration?

   _____

2. Where did this event take place? Be specific.

   _____

3. Draw a sketch of the scene where it took place as you remember it:

   [ ]

4. How old were you at the time?_____

5. Who else was there with you? _____

6. Why was this holiday or celebration so special? _____

Write It! On a separate paper, write your "chapter" about this special holiday or celebration. Use dialogue, action, and descriptive details to make the event and your feelings as real for your readers as Laura Ingalls Wilder did in Chapter 19 of *Little House on the Prairie.*

Quiz Time!

1. On the back of this paper, write a one-paragraph summary of the major events that happen in each of the chapters in this section. Then complete the questions on the rest of this page.

2. When Pa went to Independence to get the seeds and plow, he brought back several things the Ingalls family considered luxuries, things they did not really need. What were they?

_____

_____

3. What were the first signs that something unusual was going on among the Indians?

_____

4. How did Pa and Ma save their house from the prairie fire?

_____

5. How did the prairie animals save themselves from the fire?

_____

6. How had Jack changed? Why?

_____

_____

7. How could you tell that Pa was really worried about what the Indians were going to do?

_____

_____

8. What did the Indians quarrel about?

_____

9. Why did Pa decide to leave the little house on the prairie?

_____

10. What do the Indians and the Ingalls family have in common at the end of the book?

_____

_____

Little Garden on the Window Ledge

Pa said the family would be "living like kings" once their garden was growing. The family was especially looking forward to the garden vegetables after a long winter of mostly meat and bread. Some of Ma's garden was planted with seeds started in the house. Some of the garden was started by planting seeds directly in the ground, while some plants in Ma's garden were started from vegetables saved for planting. Try one or more of the following methods for yourself.

Sprouting Seeds for Planting

Put bean or corn seeds on a small plate or Styrofoam tray covered with a wet paper towel. Set in a sunny place. Keep the paper towel moist. Watch for the seeds to sprout. Plant the sprouted seeds in a dirt-filled pot or paper cup. Keep track of how long it takes the seeds to sprout and for the planted sprouts to grow into healthy plants.

Planting Seeds in a Pot

Plant seeds directly into a dirt-filled pot or cup. Keep the pot or cup in a sunny place and the dirt moist. Keep track of how long it takes for the shoots to show through the dirt and for healthy plants to grow from the seeds. Compare this to the time it took to sprout the seeds and then plant them (as above).

Seeds from Vegetables

Cut a 1" (2.54 cm) piece from the top (the larger end with the leaf stem) of a carrot. Plant, stem upward, in a dirt-filled pot. Keep the pot in a sunny place and the dirt moist. Keep track of how long it takes for a new carrot plant to grow.

Or

Set aside a potato until sprouts begin to form on the outside. Plant the potato in a dirt-filled pot. Keep the pot in a sunny place and the dirt moist. Keep track of how long it takes for a new potato plant to grow.

Fire!

There are several incidents involving fire in *Little House on the Prairie*. Pa takes special care in building their campfire so they do not set fire to the prairie grass. Ma must watch her cooking fire so it doesn't set fire to the canvas roof of the cabin. A prairie fire threatens the family and their home and animals. The chimney catches fire, and Laura saves Mary and Carrie.

Fire prevention and control are just as important today as they were in Laura's time, but the way fires are prevented and controlled are very different. Working together, list the prevention, causes, and emergency actions involved with the fires in *Little House on the Prairie*. Then, use a book or interview a fire-prevention expert (a local firefighter, for example) to fill in the same information about the prevention, causes, and emergency actions involved in fires today.

FIRE!		
ITEM	**IN *LITTLE HOUSE* BOOK**	**TODAY**
Prevention		
Causes		
Emergency Actions		

Geronimo!

In *Little House on the Prairie*, the Indian leader Soldat du Chene convinced the Osage Indians that they should not fight against the white settlers and soldiers. Do some research to find out about an Indian leader who decided to fight and was the last of his people to surrender. Look up Geronimo in a book or encyclopedia and answer these questions:

1. To what tribe did Geronimo belong? _____

2. Where did this tribe live? _____

3. Why did Geronimo lead his people in revolts against the United States government? _____

    _____

    _____

4. What happened to him? _____

    _____

5. What happened to his people, those who had not joined in his revolt?

    _____

    _____

Consider and Decide: If you had been a Native American leader during the time Soldat du Chene and Geronimo led their people, what would you have advised them to do? Why?

Speak Up! Write the speech (2–3 minutes) you would have given to your people as you advised them to leave their land, go peacefully to the reservation, revolt against the United States, or whatever you would urge them to do. Practice the speech and present it to the class.

Details, Details!

In Chapter 23 of *Little House on the Prairie*, Laura Ingalls Wilder uses a variety of details to build the suspense and create a fearful mood. Below is one example of each type of detail she used — sounds, actions, feelings and thoughts, and dialogue. Try to find one or two more examples of each type of suspense and mood-building detail. Write the examples on the lines.

SOUNDS	Example: savage voices shouting _____ _____ _____
ACTIONS	Example: Pa brought Jack into the house. _____ _____ _____
FEELINGS/ THOUGHTS	Example: Laura had a feeling something was watching her, creeping up behind her. _____ _____ _____
DIALOGUE	Example: Pa says, "My mouth's so dry, I couldn't whistle a tune to save my life." _____ _____ _____

Discuss: Was this fear justified? What emotions do you think the Indians were feeling?

Write: Write about a time you were afraid, or make up a story involving a child like you in a scary situation. Use a variety of details to build suspense and create a scary mood.

"The Only Good Indian"

Look up the word *prejudice* in a dictionary. Then, in your own words, write a definition here:

_____

_____

_____

Work in groups of two to four students to discuss and then answer these questions:

1. How do some of the characters in *Little House on the Prairie* show their prejudice against the Indians? Write the name of the character followed by what he/she does or says that shows this prejudice.

Character	*Act of Prejudice*	

2. Find proof that this prejudice is not justified. (Use details in the book to show that these ideas about the Indians are not entirely correct.) Write your responses on the back of this paper.

3. On the back of this paper, make a group list of examples of the prejudices people show today. Then, as a group, decide what might be the best way(s) to overcome such prejudices.

Any Questions?

When you finished reading *Little House on the Prairie*, did you have some questions that were left unanswered? Write them here.

_____

_____

_____

_____

Work alone or in groups to prepare possible answers for the questions you have asked above or for some of those written below. When you have finished, share your ideas with the class.

- What do you think the Ingalls family did after they left the little house on the prairie?

- What do you think happened to the Indians who rode by Laura's house?

- Laura was fascinated by the Indian children. What did Laura have in common with those children? How was her life different from theirs?

- Do you think the Ingalls family should have left the little house on the prairie?

- Do you think the Ingalls family will ever see Mr. Edwards or their relatives again?

- Laura thinks of herself as being very naughty. What do you think?

- Would you have made a good pioneer? Why or why not?

- How does what Laura's family needs to feel contented differ from what families today think they need to be happy?

- Which character did you admire the most? Why?

- Was Soldat du Chene right or wrong in opposing the other Indian tribes who wanted to fight the white soldiers and settlers?

- Does *Little House on the Prairie* give a fair and realistic picture of the Native Americans of the time? Why or why not?

- How do you think Jack felt about moving on again?

- Based on what you have learned from reading the book, what advice would you give to "tenderfeet" who might be thinking about going west?

- Which of the girls, Mary or Laura, is most like you? Which did you like better?

- What sort of personal and working relationship did Ma and Pa Ingalls have? How is this the same or different from the relationship between husbands and wives today?

- Adults in Laura's time thought "Children should be seen and not heard." Do you agree? Do adults still feel that way?

Book Report Ideas

There are numerous ways to report on a book once you have read it. After you have finished reading *Little House on the Prairie*, choose one method of reporting on the book. It may be a way that your teacher suggests, an idea of your own, or one of the ways that is mentioned below.

- **See What I Read?**

  This report is a visual one. You can create a model of a scene from the story, illustrate a scene that was not illustrated in the book, or draw or sculpt a likeness of one of the characters.

- **A Letter to and from a Character**

  You will need a partner for this report. First, you and your partner should each write a letter to the character of your choice. In your letter, ask the character why he/she did or did not do certain things, how he/she felt about what happened, etc. Then, exchange letters with your partner. Now, pretend you are the character receiving the letter your partner has written. Answer your partner's letter.

- **Dear Diary**

  Little House on the Prairie tells the story from Laura's point of view. It is very much like a diary of her experiences when her family moved to the prairie. Pretend you are one of the other characters in the book — Ma, Pa, Mary, Mr. Edwards, or the Indian Soldat du Chene. Tell about two of the incidents in the book as if you were that character, writing about the events in his/her diary.

- **Come to Life!**

  This report is one that lends itself to a group project. A size-appropriate group prepares a scene from the story for dramatization, acts it out, and relates the significance of the scene to the entire book. Costumes, props, and sound effects will add to the dramatization.

- **Coming Attraction!**

  Little House on the Prairie is about to be made into a movie, and you have been chosen to design the promotional poster. Include the title and the author of the book, a listing of the main characters and the actors who will play them, a drawing of a scene from the book, and a paragraph synopsis of the story.

- **Into the Future**

  This report predicts what might happen if *Little House on the Prairie* were to continue. It may take the form of a story in narrative or dramatic form, or a visual display.

- **Read, Watch, Compare**

  The book, *Little House on the Prairie*, was the basis of a very popular TV series by the same name. Many episodes of the series are available on video tape. Watch an episode of the TV show, then prepare an oral or written report on the similarities and differences between the book and television versions, comparing things like setting, the house and furnishings, the clothing, the characters and their personalities, etc.

Research Ideas

Describe three things you read in *Little House on the Prairie* about which you would like to learn more.

1. _____

2. _____

3. _____

As you were reading *Little House on the Prairie*, you encountered historical information, a different and difficult way of life, diverse people, cultures and geographic regions, and a variety of animals. To increase your understanding of the characters and events in the story, as well as recognize more fully Laura Ingalls Wilder's craft as a writer, research to find out more about these people, places, and things.

Work in groups to research one or more of the areas you named above, or the areas that are mentioned below. Share your findings with the rest of the class in any appropriate form of oral presentation.

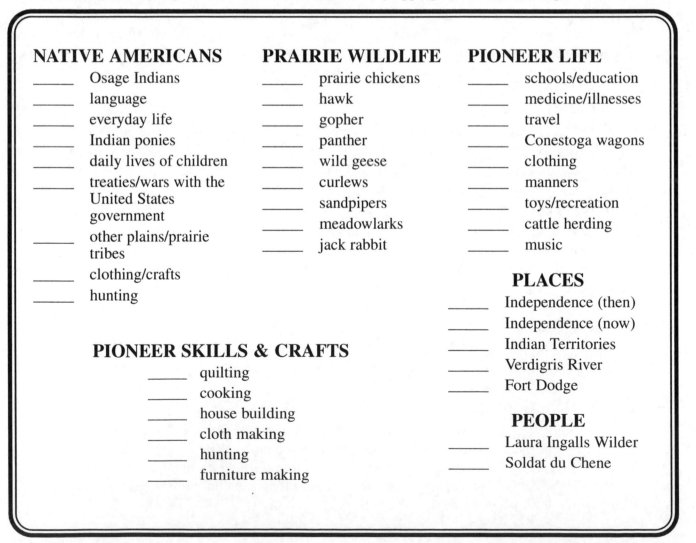

NATIVE AMERICANS
- _____ Osage Indians
- _____ language
- _____ everyday life
- _____ Indian ponies
- _____ daily lives of children
- _____ treaties/wars with the United States government
- _____ other plains/prairie tribes
- _____ clothing/crafts
- _____ hunting

PIONEER SKILLS & CRAFTS
- _____ quilting
- _____ cooking
- _____ house building
- _____ cloth making
- _____ hunting
- _____ furniture making

PRAIRIE WILDLIFE
- _____ prairie chickens
- _____ hawk
- _____ gopher
- _____ panther
- _____ wild geese
- _____ curlews
- _____ sandpipers
- _____ meadowlarks
- _____ jack rabbit

PIONEER LIFE
- _____ schools/education
- _____ medicine/illnesses
- _____ travel
- _____ Conestoga wagons
- _____ clothing
- _____ manners
- _____ toys/recreation
- _____ cattle herding
- _____ music

PLACES
- _____ Independence (then)
- _____ Independence (now)
- _____ Indian Territories
- _____ Verdigris River
- _____ Fort Dodge

PEOPLE
- _____ Laura Ingalls Wilder
- _____ Soldat du Chene

Pros & Cons

Would you want a house on the prairie? Pa says the prairie is a great place to settle. As you read the book *Little House on the Prairie*, you learned about many of the advantages of settling there. However, you learned about many disadvantages of settling the prairie as well. Working together in groups of two or three, list below the **Pros** (advantages) and **Cons** (disadvantages) of settling on the prairie back when the Ingalls family lived there.

PROS	CONS

Let's Debate

In a debate, two people (or two groups) with different opinions discuss an issue or problem. One person (or group) tries to show that his opinion is right and the other person's (or group's) opinion is wrong. One of the issues in *Little House on the Prairie* is who should own the land. Laura keeps saying that it is Indian land, and at the end of the book, the government is giving it back to the Indians. Pa and Mr. Scott think that the land should belong to the settlers. There are reasons and facts to support both sides. List as many of those reasons and facts as you can below:

The Indians Should Own It	The Settlers Should Own It

Ready, Set, Debate!

1. Decide which opinion you think is right.

2. Get together with the others in your class who feel the same as you do.

3. Put together all your reasons into one list.

4. Debate the issue with your classmates who have chosen the other side of the issue.

You Don't Say!

Some of the sayings we use today have been around a long time. You may have heard your parents or grandparents use some of the same expressions Ma and Pa used in *Little House on the Prairie*. Some of Ma's and Pa's sayings are listed below. Explain what you think each saying means:

1. "All's well that ends well."

_____

_____

2. "Little pitchers have big ears."

_____

_____

3. "Better safe than sorry."

_____

_____

4. "We'll cross that bridge when we come to it."

_____

_____

5. "It's an ill wind that doesn't blow some good."

_____

_____

6. "A miss is as good as a mile."

_____

_____

Write About It: On a separate paper, write about a time when one of the expressions above would have fit something that happened to you or someone you know.

How'd You Do That?

In *Little House on the Prairie*, Laura Ingalls Wilder gives very specific descriptions of how certain things were done. In the space below, write or illustrate, in order, the steps involved in doing one of these things:

A. Building the walls of a house   D. Laying a puncheon floor

B. Putting on a roof   E. Fighting a prairie fire

C. Putting up a door   F. Digging a well

HOW TO

How do you do that? Although they may seem hard or complicated to us, the tasks above were just common chores to the pioneers. Think of something you do all the time that would seem hard or complicated to the Ingalls family (like programming your VCR, writing an essay on a computer, riding a bicycle, cooking something in the microwave, etc.). Write a paragraph or two explaining how to do this task. Try to be as detailed and specific as Laura Ingalls Wilder was.

Unit Test

Matching: Match each pioneer tool or device with what it was used for.

1. _____ picket line
2. _____ iron spider
3. _____ auger
4. _____ sadiron
5. _____ windlass
6. _____ latch string
7. _____ bootjack

a. heated and used to press wrinkles from clothes

b. notched wood used to pull off boots.

c. used to lift things, like a bucket from a well

d. used to open a door from the outside; kept inside for security at night

e. rope and stake used to allow animals to graze without wandering loose

f. pot with legs to hold it up over a cooking fire

g. used to bore holes in wood

True or False: Write *true* or *false* next to each statement below. On the back of this paper, explain why each *false* answer is false.

1. _____ Mary was Laura's younger sister.

2. _____ The Ingalls family's fever was caused by eating watermelons.

3. _____ Laura did not really want to give her beads to her baby sister.

4. _____ Laura never got to see the Indian papoose she wanted to see.

5. _____ Pa had great respect for Soldat du Chene.

6. _____ The Osage Indians led the fight against the white settlers.

7. _____ The Ingalls were the only settlers in their area who decided to leave the Indian Territory.

8. _____ The Ingalls children had a lot of friends to play with.

Short Answer: Write a short answer for each of these questions.

1. In what present-day state was the little house on the prairie? _____

2. Who were Jack and Patty? _____

3. To whom did Pa give the cow and calf? _____

4. Who killed the panther? _____

5. Who saved the Ingalls family when they nearly died of the fever? _____

Essay: Answer these questions on the back of this paper.

1. How did pioneer neighbors help one another?

2. What skills and qualities did it take to make a good pioneer?

3. Tell why you think Laura is more like her mother or her father.

Response

Explain the meaning of each of these quotations from *Little House on the Prairie.*

Chapters 1–2:   *That prairie looked as if no human eye had ever seen it before.*

Chapters 3–4:   *The Indians would not be here long. Pa had word from a man in Washington that the Indian Territory would be open to settlement soon.*

Chapters 5–6:   *"No matter how thick and close the neighbors get, this country'll never feel crowded. Look at that sky!"*

Chapter 7:   *"But my gun would have been no use if I'd had it."*

Chapter 8:   *"A man doesn't need nails to build a house or make a door."*

Chapters 9–10:   *"I've never been beholden to any man yet, and I never will be."*

Chapter 11:   *"Do as you're told," said Pa, "and no harm will come to you."*

Chapter 12:   *"I might as well be a snake, the way I keep on shedding my skin in this country."*

Chapters 13–14:   *Her chest felt all hot inside, and she wished with all her might that Mary wouldn't always be such a good little girl.*

Chapters 15–16:   *Laura was too scared to think.*

Chapters 17–18:   *"Land knows, they'd never do anything with this country themselves."*

Chapters 19–20:   *They had never even thought of such a thing as having a penny.*

Chapters 21–22:   *"I tell you, Caroline, when we begin getting crops off this rich land of ours, we'll be living like kings!"*

Chapters 23–24:   *"If we need one, we'd need it before we could get it built. And the last thing we want to do is act like we're afraid."*

Chapter 25:   *"No, Scott!" Pa answered him. "I'll not stay here to be taken away by the soldiers like an outlaw!"*

Chapter 26:   *"Tenderfeet!" he said again. "Shouldn't be allowed loose west of the Mississippi!"*

Teacher Note: Choose an appropriate number of quotes for your students.

Conversations

Work in groups to write and perform the conversations that might have occurred in the following situations:

- Laura and Mary say good-bye to their grandparents in Wisconsin. (4 people)

- Pa explains to Mary and Laura why they have to leave the Big Woods. (3 people)

- The French-speaking Indian who visits the Ingalls' cabin tells his wife and children about the family of settlers he has met. (4 people)

- Pa and Mr. Edwards meet and come to an agreement to exchange work and help each other build their houses. (2 people)

- One or two of the cowboys whom Pa helped with the cattle herding come to the cabin for dinner with the Ingalls family. (5 or 6 people)

- Mr. Scott and Mr. Edwards come to tell Pa that the government intends to m⋯⋯ ⋯ off the land they have settled. (3 people)

- Ma and Mr. Scott talk about how they feel about having to leave ⋯ ⋯ir land and move again. (2 people)

- Mr. Edwards meets Santa Claus, who asks him to take the gifts to Laura and Mary. (2 people)

- In sign language and pantomime, Pa tells the Indian w⋯o killed the panther about his own encounter with the pack of wolves. (2 people)

- Laura gets to meet and talk to an Indian boy or g⋯ l who is about her own age. (2 people)

- One or two other Indian leaders try to convinc⋯ Soldat du Chene that he is wrong about not fighting the settlers. (2 or 3 people)

- Pa and Ma explain to Mary and Laura why they will have to leave the little house on the prairie. (4 people)

- Mary and Laura (keep their different personalities in mind) talk about how they feel about leaving the little house on the prairie and moving again. (2 people)

- Jack, Patty, and Pet discuss their roles in the lives of the Ingalls family. (3 people)

- Pa answers Ma's, Laura's, and Mary's questions about the trip to Independence when he brought back the combs for their hair. (4 people)

Bibliography

Related Reading:

Anderson, William. *Laura Ingalls Wilder: A Biography.* Harper Collins, 1992.

Walker, Barbara. *The Little House Cookbook: Frontier Foods from Laura Ingalls Wilder's Classic Stories.* Harper and Row, 1979.

The following is a partial listing of the other works of Laura Ingalls Wilder: (1953 editions illustrated by Garth Williams)

Farmer Boy. Harper, 1953.

Little House in the Big Woods. Harper, 1932, 1953.

Little Town on the Prairie. Harper, 1941, 1953.

The Long Winter. Harper, 1940, 1953.

On the Banks of Plum Creek. Harper, 1937, 1953.

Those Happy, Golden Years. Harper, 1940, 1953.

Other fiction books about life on the prairie:

Brink, Carol Ryrie. *Caddie Woodlawn.* Macmillan, 1935, 1973.

Conrad, Pam. *My Daniel.* Harper and Row, 1989.

Harvey, Brett. *Cassie's Journey: Going West in the 1860's.* Holiday House, 1988.

Harvey, Brett. *My Prairie Christmas.* Holiday House, 1990.

Hooks, William. *Pioneer Cat.* Random House, 1988.

Lasky, Kathryn. *Beyond the Divide.* Macmillan, 1983.

MacLachlan, Patricia. *Sarah, Plain and Tall.* Harper and Row, 1985.

Nonfiction Books About Pioneer Life:

Bial, Raymond. *Frontier Home.* Houghton Mifflin, 1993.

Hirschi, Ron. *Who Lives on ... the Prairie?* Putnam, 1989.

Laycock, George and Ellen. *How the Settlers Lived.* David McKay, 1980.

Related Novels About Native American Children:

Hudson, Jan. *Sweetgrass.* Philomel, 1989.

O'Dell, Scott. *Sing Down the Moon.* Houghton Mifflin, 1970.

Speare, Elizabeth George. *The Sign of the Beaver.* Houghton Mifflin, 1983.

Answer Key

Page 10
1. Accept appropriate answers.
2. It was too crowded.
3. They were too heavy to take in the wagon. They could make new ones.
4. They had to cross before the frozen lake began to thaw.
5. Answers will vary, including: tether, feed and water the horses, make the beds, cook the dinner, clean the dishes, help the girls get ready for bed.
6. He made slats and pulled the wood up over the slats.
7. An old trail
8. A. the horses
   B. the neighbor who helped Pa build the house
   C. the dog
9. Spitting tobacco
10. Answers will vary.

Page 11
1. Have a set destination and a house waiting for them
2. Travel by car, plane, moving van, etc.
3. Take all their belongings
4. Make the trip in days or hours
5. Sleep in motels
6. Eat at restaurants
7. Use laundromats or their own washers, etc., when they get to their new home
8. Face car accidents, flat tires, etc.
9. Have modern highways and maps
10. See lots of other people on the way

Page 15
1. Accept reasonable answers.
2. A. Mr. & Mrs. Scott, 3 miles.
   B. Two bachelors, 9 miles.
3. They built it half on each property.
4. Taller than Mary. Pointed ears. Curled tail. Shaggy gray coat. Green eyes.
5. Mud. Clay and water.
6. What: It is a method of cutting notches into saplings, laying them up like walls of the house and plastering them with mud. It was easier than trying to get heavy stones to the top of the chimney.
7. His unruly hair.
8. China woman figurine.
9. They were grateful but they hated having to borrow and be "beholden."
10. Answers will vary.

Page 17
Answers will vary.

Page 18
Compare to map of Midwestern US.

Page 19
Answers will vary, including:
   Mary: quiet, fearful
   Laura: adventuresome/curious, brave, mischievous
   Both: obedient, helpful

Page 20
1. Accept appropriate answers.
2. So they would not harm her family.
3. Jack might have bitten the Indians and that would have caused trouble.
4. It was made from oak slabs and straw-ti
5. Pa sent a candle to see if there were ases at the bottom of the well.
6. He fainted.
7. They paid him with a a calf.
8. Because she had to them to Carrie.
9. They hot and co their bones ached, and they were very tire
10. Accept apprriate sketches.

Page 21
1. The cane goes out.
2. The cadle continues to burn.
3. Ther is insufficient oxygen.
4. Th oxygen in the jar is used up.
5. Te candle needs oxygen to burn and Pa needs xygen to breath.

Page 23
nswers will vary depending on research.

Page 25
1. Accept reasonable answers.
2. She pulled Mary and the baby away from the fire.
3. No mail delivery, post office 40 miles away, delivery took months
4. Answers will vary, including: helping to build the house, checking on the family while Pa was away and helping with the heavy chores, getting the gifts for the girls and bringing them on Christmas, loaning them the nails.
5. Glass for the windows
6. An Indian trail still in use
7. They were going to trade the furs to get the plow and seeds.

Answer Key *(cont.)*

8. Answers will vary, including: turkey dinner, stockings, gifts from Santa.
9. A panther
10. Accept all appropriate answers.

Page 28

Interview answers will vary. Ingalls family: Sprained ankle — soaked in hotwater, wrapped. Fumes — led him to lie in the fresh air. Fever — cold cloths, quinine. Cold temperature and water — warm by fire.

Page 30

1. Accept all reasonable answers.
2. White flour, coffee, pickles, calico, crackers, hair ribbons
3. Gathering of so many, war cry
4. Starting a smaller backfire, digging a ditch, beating at it with cloths
5. They went into the stream.
6. Angry and growly; doesn't like being tied up
7. Brought Jack in the house, made bullets, stayed up on guard at night
8. Whether to fight the whites or not.
9. He didn't want to be forced off like a criminal by the soldiers.
10. They were both being forced to leave their homes.

Page 32

Answers will vary. *Little House* answers may include: prevention — using green wood and mud coatings on chimney. Causes — hot ash in the chimney and on the roof, Indian fire to clear the prairie land Action — beat with cloth, dig ditch, backfire

Page 33

1. Apache
2. Southwestern United States and Mexico
3. The United States government moved the Apaches to the San Carlos Reservation in Arizona.
4. The United States government moved Geronimo to Fort Sill in Oklahoma in 1894 where he lived the rest of his life.
5. The army imprisoned many peaceful Apache along with Geronimo and his followers.

Page 34

Accept any appropriate examples.

Page 35

Accept any reasonable answers.

Page 39

Answers will vary.

Page 40

Answers will vary.

Page 41

Accept reasonable interpretations of the sayings.

Page 43

Matching: 1. e, 2. f, 3. g, 4. a, 5. c, 6. d, 7. b

T/F

1. F, Mary was older.
2. F, The mosquitoes caused it.
3. T
4. F, She saw a lot of Indian children and babies when the Indians all rode by her house.
5. T
6. F, The Osage argued against fighting.
7. F, Mr. Edwards left too.
8. F, There were no other children.

Short Answer:

1. Kansas
2. dog and horse
3. Mr. Scott
4. an Indian
5. Doctor Tan

Essay:

Answers will vary.

Page 44

Accept reasonable interpretations.